P9-EES-637

THE ST MATTHEW PASSION

THE ST MATTHEW PASSION

ITS PREPARATION AND PERFORMANCE

BY

ADRIAN CEDRIC BOULT

AND

WALTER EMERY

NOVELLO AND CO LTD

160 WARDOUR STREET

LONDON W·1

FIRST PRINTED IN 1949

Set in 11 on 12 point Bembo and
printed by Page & Thomas Ltd., Chesham, and bound by
Novello & Co. Ltd., London, W.1

Made in England

CONTENTS

I	INTRODUCTION	1
II	SHORTENED VERSIONS	4
III	SCORES AND PARTS	7
IV	THE CONTINUO PART	11
V	SOLOISTS	20
VI	REHEARSAL PLANNING	23
VII	THE INDIVIDUAL MOVEMENTS	29
VIII	PROGRAMME NOTES	54
APPENDIX I	THE CHORUS *He guilty is of death*	63
APPENDIX II	NOTES FOR THE KEYBOARD PLAYERS	68
APPENDIX III	AN AUTHENTIC CONTINUO REALIZATION	71
APPENDIX IV	BOOKS FOR FURTHER READING	74

Chapter I

INTRODUCTION

THERE MUST be many choral conductors who would like nothing better than to perform the St Matthew Passion, but are afraid to attempt it. One of the objects of this book is to show that their resources may be more adequate than they think. It is true that the work is difficult; but, as is usual with Bach, its difficulties are of a special kind. It requires musicianship and hard work, not lavish expenditure and a large number of performers.

There must be enough singers to form a double choir; but a very large choir, far from being essential, is positively undesirable. All his life Bach wrote for the immediate need and the available resources; and there is no doubt that he meant the Passion to be performed as he performed it himself: with a small choir, and an orchestra of about the same size. (See Terry, *Bach: The Passions, II*, p. 11.) A choir of sixty is quite large enough; and a smaller number will suffice, especially if the work has to be performed with a reduced orchestra, since it is extremely important that the orchestra should not be overwhelmed by the choir.

As with the singers, so with the instrumentalists; the term 'double orchestra' sounds much more formidable than it is in fact. Forty or fifty players are enough: about thirty strings, four flutes, four oboes, two bassoons, a harpsichord, and an organ. (The 'obsolete' instruments in the score—recorders, oboi d'amore, and viola da gamba—can be replaced by flutes, oboes or cors anglais, and cello with so little loss of effect that they are hardly worth considering.) It is probably inadvisable to use an orchestra much larger than this, unless extra strings can be balanced by extra wind instruments, which is seldom possible. On the other hand, the numbers can easily be reduced. To begin with, one does not really need thirty strings; again, since the bassoons simply double the string basses, to dispense with them involves nothing worse than a slight loss of clarity; the oboe and flute parts can be taken by strings; and a piano can be used as a substitute for the scarce and expensive harpsichord, either with an organ, or as the only continuo instrument if an organ is not available. There is no point in discussing further reductions; it is sufficient to say that with a little ingenuity they can be made, and that it is better to perform the Passion with no accompaniment but that of a piano than not to perform it at all.

The number of solo singers required is six at the most: the Evangelist, Jesus, and a quartet to sing the lyrics and the fragments of recitative allotted to the minor characters. The expense of engaging six professionals may well be prohibitive; but much can be done by drawing on local talent, or having certain arias sung by sections of the choir. Many Bach arias demand such extraordinarily good breath-control that they are better sung by three or four voices than by any but the best soloists.

As for the length of the work—some three hours and a half—it is not too long to be performed complete in one day; and ways of shortening it will be suggested in Chapter II. Cutting necessarily involves regrettable omissions, but need not detract seriously from the general effect.

So far as material resources are concerned, therefore, the Passion makes smaller demands than it is commonly supposed to, and could certainly be performed creditably by many more choirs than attempt it at present. It does, however, present interpretative difficulties which, though no greater than those of many a Bach cantata that one would tackle without hesitation, must not be underestimated. Even those movements that are technically easy can be sung convincingly only by a choir that has caught the true Bach spirit from its conductor. For this reason some conductors may find it advisable not to produce the whole of the Passion at the first attempt, but to begin with a shortened version, a single Part, or even a few carefully selected movements—not more than can be studied with due care—and add movements year by year until the whole work can be given an adequate performance.

Chapter II

SHORTENED VERSIONS

WHETHER the work is to be performed complete or in a shortened version, the conductor must obtain a grasp of its plan ; and the easiest way to do this is to read the libretto.

The Passion is divided into two Parts, Part I lasting about one hour and thirty-five minutes, and Part II two hours. At the beginnings and ends of the two Parts stand four great choral meditations (nos 1, 35, 36, and 78) : as it were, the corner-stones of the whole work. Each Part is divided into a number of contrasted scenes, marked off by lyrics. Of the latter, those written by the librettist Picander are set as arias (usually preceded by accompanied recitatives) ; others, being verses from hymns, are set to the chorale melodies normally associated with them. These melodies were familiar to Bach's audiences, who, to judge by the scoring, joined the choir in singing them.

Once the conductor has grasped the plan of the whole work, he can decide how to cut it—if he is so unfortunate as to have to do so. He may perhaps decide to perform a single Part ; this can be done with good effect. He may retain the whole of the narrative, but omit much of the commentary provided by the arias and chorales. There are many ways in which circumstances may affect his decision ; for instance, certain aspects of the story may for some reason seem particularly important, or certain movements may have to be omitted to save a soloist. This, therefore, is a matter on which it is hardly possible to give useful advice ; but a real effort should be made to retain nos 67–73 (the Crucifixion sequence) and nos 77 and 78 (the solo portions of no. 77 can quite well be sung by sections of the choir, if four soloists are not available). The other three cornerstones (nos 1, 35, and 36) should all be included, if possible ; but there is room for differences of opinion. No. 35 is extremely difficult, and may have to be omitted (as in Sir Walford Davies' abridgement) for this reason. Conductors who find themselves unable to include it should consider replacing it by the alternative provided in the latest issues of the Elgar-Atkins vocal score (see p. 40).

Here are details of three shortened versions. All the references are to the numbering in the Elgar-Atkins edition.

1. *Duration about 2 hrs 20 mins*

This version was planned by Sir Steuart Wilson ; it reduces the work to the length of an ordinary concert.

Omit the following movements and passages :
6–10, 20, 21, 27–31 : 32, bars 1–15 : 37–41, 48–53, 55–58 : 59, omit the second recitative and chorus : 61 : 64, bar 6 to end : 65, 66, 70 : 73, from the first chord of bar 21 to the second chord of bar 30 : 74, 75 : 76, bar 8 to end.

2. *Duration about 2 hrs 45 mins*

This version was used by Sir Walford Davies for many of his performances in Wales.

Omit the following movements and passages :
6–10, 13, 14 : 15, bars 1–9 : 29 : 34, bars 1–16 : 35, 36, 41 : 50, last ten bars : 52, 61, 66 : 73, bar 21 to end : 74, 75, 76.

He occasionally made a longer cut : nos 48–52. This saves about another seven minutes.

3. *Duration about 2 hrs 5 mins*

This is the abridgement made for St Paul's Cathedral.

Omit the following movements and passages :
12, 27–29, 34–36 : 37, bars 6–16 : 38–41, 48–53 : 54, bars 8–21 : 57–8, 61–9, 75 : 76, bars 1–11.

Abridgements should, however, be regarded as stepping-stones. The conductor's ultimate aim must be to perform the work complete—except, perhaps, for the Da Capos, some of which are nearly always shortened. Most conductors probably find that as time goes on they play more and more of them in full ; and in any case, discretion is necessary. Not every aria can be satisfactorily rounded off by a mere repetition of its opening ritornello.

When a complete performance is given in one day, it is wise to have a break of about two hours between the two Parts. At the Bach Choir performances on Passion Sunday Part I is played from 11 to 12.40, and Part II from 2.30 to 4.30. A good alternative arrangement is to begin Part I at 3.30, and Part II at 7.30.

Chapter III

SCORES AND PARTS

Vocal Scores

THE FOLLOWING complete editions of the vocal score, with English words, have been published:

LAMBORN COCK & CO., 1862. Folio. Edited by Sterndale Bennett.

NOVELLO, 1870. The same, in octavo.

NOVELLO, 1894. Retranslated by Troutbeck.

STAINER & BELL, 1910. Edited by Stanford for a performance he conducted at the Leeds Festival in 1910.

PAXTON, 1922. This edition is based on that of Sterndale Bennett, but partly retranslated by various hands. It contains sol-fa, and Sir Walford Davies found it useful in Wales.

In all the above editions, as in the St Paul's Cathedral abridgement, the translations are to some extent bowdlerized.

BREITKOPF, 1906. This edition suffers somewhat from the translator's rigid adherence to the Gospel words.

In the lyrical portions of the Passion the translator's task, though by no means easy, is at any rate straightforward: he has to find English words to fit Bach's notes. But this does not apply to the Gospel passages. A translation that fitted Bach's notes would be so very unbiblical that it would jar on English ears; *Lass ihn kreuzigen,* for instance, would become *Have Him crucified,* instead of the familiar *Let Him be crucified.* On the other hand, retention of the Gospel words involves drastic alteration of Bach's notes, which is equally unacceptable. It is therefore generally agreed that in these passages the translator must compromise : the best translation is that which most tactfully reconciles the opposed claims of the English words and Bach's music.

NOVELLO, 1911. Edited by Elgar and Sir Ivor Atkins. This was at once recognized as the standard edition for English use. It is, however, no longer in print, having been superseded by

NOVELLO, 1938. The music text of this edition embodies some changes that were made in later issues of the 1911 edition, and the translation is largely new, Sir Ivor Atkins having found it possible to keep closer to Bach's notes, while still retaining a Biblical flavour, by making use of various sixteenth-century translations of the Bible.

The differences between the editions of 1911 and 1938 are almost confined to the solo parts ; but the choir is affected by the revised translation on pp. 32 (no. 16), 73, 105–6, 118, and 147. Conductors must therefore see that all their singers are using the same edition. The 1938 translation is preferable, except perhaps at pp. 105–6 (see Chapter VII and Appendix I).

Full Scores

Conductors should make sure that the scores they use —whether miniature scores for study, or full scores for the actual performance—give Bach's own orchestration. Modernized orchestration, as in the version by Franz, may have done good service in its day ; but there is no excuse for it now.

As the full scores available on hire from Messrs Novello are Bach-Gesellschaft copies, pasted up to conform with the Elgar-Atkins vocal score, conductors will find it convenient to make themselves acquainted with this edition ; but the Peters and Eulenburg scores will serve equally well for practical purposes. Those who enjoy solving textual problems will find much to interest them in the differences between the facsimile of Bach's original full score (Insel-Verlag, Leipzig 1922), the Bach-Gesellschaft edition, and the edition by Max Schneider (Breitkopf, 1937).

Orchestral Parts

A great deal of time can be wasted at rehearsal over inconsistent section lettering and dynamic marks in hired orchestral material; the conductor should, and indeed must, attend to these matters himself beforehand. In themselves, the Novello hired parts will give him no trouble; though if he adopts some of the suggestions made in Chapter VII, he will have to alter the dynamic marks here and there. He should, however, be on his guard against the confusing and contradictory pencilled marks that some unprincipled users leave in the parts. A large indiarubber is an essential item of a conductor's stock-in-trade—for removing his own marks as well as other people's.

When hired parts are being ordered, the following points should be borne in mind, particularly if the work is being performed in a shortened version or with a reduced orchestra.

Bach's two orchestras answer each other like the two choirs, though they unite in the chorales and occasionally elsewhere. They sit separately, and therefore have separate parts; and as the solos are accompanied by either Orchestra I or Orchestra II, but not both, the parts for both orchestras must be obtained.

If the leader of Orchestra II is not a good soloist, his important obbligato in no. 51 can be played by the leader of Orchestra I. This must be arranged beforehand, since an extra part will be required.

In nos 40, 41, 65, and 66 Bach wrote for a viola da gamba. A part for that instrument can be obtained ; but a cello adaptation is almost invariably used, and is quite satisfactory. Neither form of the obbligati in nos 40, 65, and 66 is included in the orchestral cello parts ; a separate part is required, whether for cello or gamba, and when he is ordering parts the conductor should state which instrument he is using.

In no. 25 there are parts for two recorders. They are usually played by flutes. If recorders are used, they will play from flute parts of Orchestra I ; and two extra parts had better be obtained.

For the flute obbligato in no. 36, see p. 41.

Bach wrote for four oboists, two in each orchestra. All four of them could play the oboe d'amore as well, and two of them (those of Orchestra I) the oboe da caccia.

The oboe da caccia obbligati are in nos 25, 57, 58, 69, 70, and 75. They can all be played on the cor anglais, and the Novello parts are transposed for that instrument.

The oboe d'amore obbligati are in nos 18, 19, 35, 36, and 45. They can be played on ordinary oboes, except for a few low notes in nos 19, 36, and 45. For no. 36 see p. 41. The parts in nos 19 and 45 can be played by a cor anglais, or the ordinary oboe can use the alternative notes provided in the parts.

In terms of modern instruments, therefore, four oboists are required for a complete performance. Two of them (those of Orchestra I) must of necessity be prepared to play the cor anglais as well, and it will be an advantage if Oboe II of Orchestra II can do so.

If oboi d'amore are available, special parts can be obtained for them.

Chapter IV

THE CONTINUO PART

EXPERIENCE suggests that some conductors still underestimate the importance of the figured continuo part. It should be clearly understood that a keyboard instrument is a normal constituent of a Bach orchestra, and an essential part of Bach's orchestral thinking, not to be omitted without most careful consideration.

Nevertheless, conditions having changed since 1729, there are one or two places in the Passion where it is possible to defend the omission of the keyboard instrument. Nowadays, for instance, it is seldom safe to encourage an audience to join in the singing of the plain chorales. Bach's heavy accompaniment of full orchestra and organ is therefore unnecessary, and when the words call for quiet treatment there is much to be said for omitting either the orchestra or the organ, or even letting the choir sing unaccompanied. Omission of the organ generally involves the loss of a few harmony notes (e.g., in the last line of no. 53 there will be no seventh at the word 'rise') ; but in the plain chorales the losses are of no great importance : the notes in question do not contribute much harmonic colour.

Again, the choral sections of no. 25 are accompanied by strings and organ. Bach's choir would perhaps have gone out of tune if left unsupported ; but nowadays a choir that could not sing these passages unaccompanied would hardly attempt the Passion at all, and it is reasonable to lighten the accompaniment. Conductors must nevertheless examine the figuring, and ensure that the harmony notes are preserved ; for here there are some that matter. See p. 37.

It is probably inadvisable to omit the keyboard instrument elsewhere, except in no. 58, where Bach did not want it. There is indeed a temptation to use it only here and there in movements such as no. 47, where the obbligati, so long as they are in action,* provide what looks like a complete accompaniment. But to bring the harpsichord or organ in only where the obbligati rest would produce abrupt changes of tone-colour and detract from the homogeneity of the movement; the keyboard instrument must play for at least a bar or two before and after the rests. What is more, even where the obbligati are harmonically complete according to textbook notions, they may not provide the entire harmonic structure as Bach conceived it. In Exx. 1 and 2 the small notes, which are among those required by the figuring, are not supplied by the obbligati; and Ex. 3 shows, at the star, a loss of a different and puzzling kind.

Realizations on Orchestral Instruments

Attempts have been made to dispense with the organ or harpsichord by working the figuring out for orchestral instruments. The result is that what Bach intended to be a background of fundamental harmony takes on obbligato status: the consecutives that constantly occur between the obbligati and the realization, harmless so long as the latter is played on a keyboard instrument and remains in the background, immediately become objectionable†: and the not infrequent clashes between obbligati and realization become unduly conspicuous. Thus, the practice leads to serious falsification of Bach's intentions.

* They rest at the main cadences—perhaps to facilitate rallentandos—and for a few beats elsewhere.

† They can be avoided, if at all, only by making the realization absurdly angular.

Conductors should not indulge in it themselves, and should avoid any edition that has been prepared in this way.

Organ or Harpsichord?

There has been much dispute about whether Bach used organ alone, or both organ and harpsichord, in his concerted church music. His views may well have changed during his twenty years of cantata-production at Leipzig, and at each performance of the Passion his decision must have been influenced by the state of repair of the available instruments and the competence of their players. The one thing that seems reasonably certain is that conductors are free to decide for themselves how to treat each movement. Organ and harpsichord can be used simultaneously, as at the Amsterdam performances under Mengelberg, where their parts were identical in many movements. The effect was excellent : that of a single instrument possessing both the characteristic impact of the harpsichord and the sustaining power of the organ. On the other hand, they can be used separately, as in the list of recommendations in Appendix II (p. 68). The choice of instrument must be made on grounds of ordinary musical effectiveness. The harpsichord is too weak to be used alone in choruses, and, owing to its evanescent tone, is unsuitable when the string basses have long notes, as in the 'Eli' passages of no. 71. (For accompanying passages in *recitativo secco* it is perhaps best used alone—that is, without string basses.) The organ is unsuitable for strikingly rhythmical movements, since it cannot produce accent and is difficult to synchronize with the orchestra* ; it is most effective for sustained chords that do not change quickly.

Use of the Organ

The organ has an extremely important part to play in any performance of the Passion ; and conductors should take care that it is used effectively.

The organist should not be asked to play rapid bass passages with the pedals. Such passages, often practically

* Organ pipes do not speak instantaneously ; and very often it is impossible for the choir and orchestra to be anywhere near the pipes themselves.

unplayable, are almost always unclear and therefore ineffective.

The effect of a good 32-foot stop is very fine ; but it can easily be overdone, and not every 32-foot stop is a good one. Furthermore, the effect requires time to develop. These stops should be reserved for long-held notes ; they are thrown away on detached crotchets, and with a moving bass they simply produce confusion.

It is very seldom advisable to reinforce any upper orchestral part by doubling it literally on the organ. On the other hand, it is often effective to give the organist a simplified (more sustained) version of an orchestral part, especially the bass. He can, for instance, hold a low E with the pedals for the first five bars of no. 1, and thereafter play dotted crotchets and dotted minims so far as possible (he should, of course, play chords on the manuals as well). In bar 6, and wherever else quaver movement is essential, it will most probably be best if he does not play the bass—not, at any rate, with the pedals— ; but much depends on the organ and its position, and the conductor must experiment for himself. Again, the organist can add depth to no. 47 by playing a sustained version of the bass, in dotted crotchets and longer notes ; and he can make movements like no. 40 sound more continuous by playing sustained chords, mostly in semibreves and minims.

Piano or Harpsichord?

Tovey went so far as to say that the piano makes a better continuo instrument than the harpsichord, because it blends less well and therefore keeps the harmonic background more distinct from the obbligati. Many will disagree with him ; but it must be admitted that a piano is better than a weak-toned harpsichord—and some harpsichords are very weak indeed. Moreover, they are still scarce, and the expense of obtaining one may well be prohibitive. In such circumstances, no-one need hesitate to use a piano.

Nevertheless, it is important to remember that Bach did not write for the piano ; and that is why the word occurs so seldom in this book. The two instruments are so different that a pianist, in exploiting his resources, may easily slip into an anachronistic style of playing.

For accompanying passages in *recitativo secco* the piano, like the harpsichord, is perhaps best used alone—that is, without string basses.

The Realization Itself

There remains the question of the actual notes to be played on the keyboard instruments. This would be easy enough if one could simply engage two players who specialize in continuo work, tell them which movements to play, and leave them to it ; but as there are not enough specialists to go round, most conductors will have to find out for themselves what printed material is available, and how far it is reliable.

A harpsichord part by Seiffert is published by Peters, and an organ part has been made for use with the Elgar-Atkins edition. Both these parts can be hired from Messrs Novello. In addition, the Elgar-Atkins vocal score naturally gives a realization for all movements that are accompanied by continuo alone, and small notes in other movements give some idea of the chords required when the obbligati rest. Together, these workings yield a more or less complete set of harpsichord and organ parts ; and for his first performances of the Passion a conductor could hardly do better than accept and combine them.

He must nevertheless take certain precautions, even at an early stage. The plain fact is that it is impossible to make a continuo realization that is acceptable in every detail ; it is hard enough to make one that is acceptable on the whole. Bach's figuring is incomplete. It is also partly illegible, as is evident from the discrepancies between the Bach-Gesellschaft and Schneider editions. In making a realization, therefore, one dare not put full confidence in the figuring as it appears in the standard editions ; the original MS. parts would probably be no more illuminating ; and this leads to very great difficulties when the figuring looks wrong. There is no doubt that Bach made mistakes ; but one must not assume that every clash between the obbligati and the figuring (see Ex. 3) is thus to be accounted for. A great composer's personal harmony must not be judged by text-book rules, which are based on the practice of composers in general, and are bound to be over-restrictive, since they are intended primarily to keep elementary students well within bounds. (For instance, there is an admirable rule that discourages beginners from obscuring the rhythmical structure of their phrases by using the same chord on two successive beats, of which the second is the stronger. But there are many effective examples of this practice in Bach (see the beginning of no. 47), and many more in Beethoven ; and it is mere academicism to imagine, as some have done, that what these men wrote in the days of their maturity can be improved by blue-pencilling it like a beginner's exercise.)

Thus, whenever the figuring of the standard editions gives rise to doubts, the editor of a continuo part has to make what may be a very difficult decision ; and as he is committing his work to print for the use of all and sundry, he will naturally tend to be cautious and academic.

For these reasons, the available continuo workings

contain a number of disputable interpretations. They are also incomplete (that is, they leave certain passages of figuring unrealized), in all probability too thin, and very occasionally too contrapuntal. One or two such points are referred to below, but only as examples of the sort of thing that is to be looked for. A long list of the dubious passages would be out of place in a book of this kind, and to discuss even some of them would occupy an unreasonable amount of space ; besides, it would lead to no very definite conclusions, for these are matters that every conductor must settle for himself. As they gain experience, therefore, conductors should check the realizations they are using against the figuring ; if their performances then fail to carry out Bach's intentions, at least that will not be due to their carelessness.

Even when the printed part undoubtedly gives the chords Bach intended, mechanical adherence to it will not yield first-class results. It is true that a certain uniformity is required in movements accompanied by continuo alone, since the singers must know what leads to expect ; but where there are obbligati, and particularly in choruses, the continuo-player should feel free to improvise—to adapt his part to the needs of the other performers from moment to moment. As a conductor gains experience with the Passion, and with Bach in general, he may well experiment in this way. He will have to write his own realizations, for two opposite reasons. On the one hand, few pianists are accustomed to work of this kind ; written-out suggestions may encourage them to improvise. On the other hand, since varied accompaniment is second nature to any competent organist, such a man, left to himself, might err in the direction of over-elaboration ; and a written part may help to keep him within bounds. As a guide to style, the conductor should examine the fragment reproduced in Appendix III—a realization by Bach himself, made for the bass aria in Cantata 3, in which there are no obbligati to add interest. The simplicity of the realization is significant. Elaborate imitative writing is evidently out of place ; little more is required than a straightforward statement of the chords implied by the figuring, generally in four parts ; of which the uppermost should move smoothly and have some slight pretensions to melodic interest.

Chapter V

SOLOISTS

FOR A PERFORMANCE of the Passion, whether complete or in any reasonable shortened version, an irreducible minimum of two good soloists is required, for the parts of Jesus and the Evangelist. How many more are required for any particular performance depends on what movements are being omitted, and how far the conductor is prepared to have arias and accompanied recitatives sung by small groups of singers from the choir. It has already been pointed out that a few good choral singers can often make Bach arias more effective than any but the very best soloists can. They can take breath unobtrusively in two or three different places, so that long phrases present no real difficulties; and if the conductor teaches them their parts, there should be no difference of conception between the singing of the arias and that of the choruses. Conductors who cannot afford good soloists for the arias should experiment on these lines without hesitation; there is probably not a single aria or accompanied recitative in the Passion that cannot be performed effectively in this way.

If funds permit, however, soloists will presumably be engaged. Six in all are required for a complete performance: the Evangelist and Jesus (who should stand on one side of the conductor, and must not sing any other parts), and a quartet of soloists for the arias and movements such as nos 33 and 77.

How far the conductor should direct the soloists is a moot point. Ideally, no doubt, every movement in the Passion should bear the impress of the same mind (the conductor's); but in practice the matter does not seem to be of great importance. The arias and accompanied recitatives convey their messages at widely differing speeds—the timings in Chapter VII show remarkable variations— ; and the vital thing surely is for the soloists to sing with complete confidence and conviction, which they are most likely to do at speeds they have arrived at themselves. It therefore does no great harm, and is probably best, to leave them alone—unless they ask for guidance or are obviously inexperienced—, the conductor simply seeing that when they have set their tempi they keep to them, except at important cadences. As for the two special roles, the conductor has little to do with the Evangelist ; and since in the part of Jesus good singers keep almost strict time, it is not difficult to accompany them.

The parts of the minor characters can be sung by members of the choir from their choral positions ; but there are drawbacks to this, not only in broadcast performances, when the distance from the microphone has to be considered, but at all times. Such soloists are often acutely nervous, for it is far worse to sing two or three isolated sentences than half a dozen arias ; they cannot be near the harpsichord, and therefore may find it difficult to sing in tune ; and they have been known to miss their cues. On the whole, if the full quartet of aria soloists is available, the conductor will do well to play for safety and get them to sing these parts, as in Table I on p. 22.

TABLE I

THE MINOR CHARACTERS

		MOVEMENT
SOPRANO	First Maid	45
	Pilate's Wife	54
CONTRALTO	First False Witness	39
	Second Maid	45
TENOR	Second False Witness	39
	First Priest	50
BASS	Judas	11, 17, 32, 49
	Peter	22, 45, 46
	High Priest	39, 42
	Second Priest	50
	Pilate	52, 54, 56, 59, 76

The False Witnesses in no. 39 may be accompanied by the organ with the string basses of Orchestra II, and the Two Priests in no. 50 by the organ with those of Orchestra I. All the other minor characters may be accompanied by the harpsichord alone.

Chapter VI

REHEARSAL PLANNING

CONDUCTORS should allow themselves ample time for choral rehearsals—all the more if the singers think themselves competent and experienced. Many of the choruses are diatonic and look easy, and, as always with Bach, it is only when one knows them well that one begins to realize how hard it is to obtain even an adequate performance. Conductors who wish to be strictly scholarly will of course use straightforward dynamic schemes, keeping more or less uniformly *piano* or *forte* for long stretches, or even throughout a chorus ; but this does not simplify matters—there is then all the more need for elaborate nuancing of the individual parts, and, in many choruses, for frequent accents and staccatos to secure vitality.

Much the same is true of amateur orchestras ; and they, like choirs, vary so much that it is useless to give detailed advice.

The following notes may be useful if a professional orchestra is being engaged, and the conductor is wondering how much rehearsal he needs. It is assumed throughout that the continuo part is divided between harpsichord and organ somewhat on the lines suggested in Appendix II.

For a rather hastily planned performance in 1946, with B.B.C. resources, there were two morning three-hour rehearsals with soloists and orchestra, and two evening rehearsals with choir and orchestra. (The Evangelist rehearsed his recitatives with the harpsichordist separately, as he must always do, for the orchestra must not be kept waiting during work on these numbers.) The morning rehearsals gave comfortable time for all the arias and the sayings of Jesus : two soloists came on one morning, and three on the other. The two evening rehearsals gave time for all the choral work, and, in addition, for rehearsing choir and soloists together in nos 25, 26, 33, 36, 70, and 77.

If the soloists are readily available, it might be better to rehearse the two orchestras separately : one each day. Rehearsals cannot be so planned that no-one wastes time ; but either of these schemes will serve as a basis.

If the conductor is confident about his choir, one rehearsal with orchestra should suffice. Indeed, it may be possible to dispense with a combined rehearsal altogether, the singers hearing the orchestra for the first time at the actual performance.

When annual performances have begun, the work soon becomes set. It has been found that after a year or two—so long as there are no great changes in the personnel of the choir and orchestra—one three-hour rehearsal is enough for the three hours and a half of music. The arias and the sayings of Jesus should be taken first. The tempi will have been determined at piano rehearsals previously, so that as a rule it will only be necessary to set the tempo of each aria, arrange the Da Capo, and give instructions for the continuo realization. (In such circumstances, lists like those given in Appendix II are of great value as time-savers.) The arias take about ninety minutes, and the part of Jesus fifteen minutes ; all this can be dealt with in seventy-five minutes of rehearsal. The choir should come at half-time. Their contributions to the work, including the choruses with soli (nos 25, 26, 33, 36, 70, and 77), amount to about seventy-five minutes ; and the essentials can be dealt with in the remaining hour and a half. The Evangelist should stay to sing the cues for the crowd choruses, so that they can be fitted in with full dramatic power. He need rehearse only these cues and those portions of nos 71 and 73 that are accompanied by organ and string basses, since he and the minor characters will have rehearsed with the harpsichordist beforehand.

If time is very short, the conductor can rehearse the part of Jesus with the strings of Orchestra I during what should be his half-time break. Then, while these strings enjoy their break, he can take one or two of the arias with Orchestra II.

The following analyses may be useful for rehearsal planning :

TABLE II

MOVEMENTS REQUIRING SOLOISTS

TENOR (EVANGELIST)	rehearses separately with harpsichord, except for parts of nos 71 and 73, in which he is accompanied by the organ and string basses of Orchestra I.
BASS (JESUS)	takes part in nos 2, 8, 15, 17, 20, 22, 24, 27, 30, 32, 34, 42, 52 (all with the organ and full strings of Orchestra I) ; and 71 (with the organ and string basses of Orchestra I).

SOPRANO	with	Orchestra I	18, 19, 33, 57, 58, 77
		Orchestra II	12
CONTRALTO		Orchestra I	9, 10, 33, 36, 47, 69, 70, 77
		Orchestra II	60, 61

TABLE II *continued*

TENOR	Orchestra I	25, 26, 77
	Orchestra II	40, 41
BASS	Orchestra I	65, 66, 74, 75, 77
	Orchestra II	28, 29, 51

For the narrative passages sung by the four aria soloists see Table I.

TABLE III

ARIAS AND ACCOMPANIED RECITATIVES WITH ORCHESTRA I

OBBLIGATI

9 Two Flutes
10 Two Flutes
18 Two Oboi d'Amore (ordinary oboes)
19 Two Oboi d'Amore (one oboe, one cor anglais)
47 Solo Violin and Full Strings
57 Two Oboi da Caccia (cors anglais)
58 One Flute and two Oboi da Caccia (no strings or keyboard instrument)
65 Two Flutes and Viola da Gamba (cello)
66 Viola da Gamba (cello)
69 Two Oboi da Caccia (cors anglais)
74 Full Strings
75 Full Strings, with the Violins doubled by two Oboi da Caccia (cors anglais)

TABLE IV

ARIAS AND ACCOMPANIED RECITATIVES WITH ORCHESTRA II

OBBLIGATI

12 Two Flutes and Strings
28 Full Strings
29 Strings without Violas
40 Two Oboes and Viola da Gamba (cello).
41 No obbligati ; the bass is played by the Viola da Gamba or one Cello
51 Solo Violin and Full Strings
60 Full Strings
61 Strings without Violas

Except no. 58, all the movements in Tables III and IV require a string bass—anything from one cello to full cellos and basses—and a keyboard instrument. Recommendations will be found in Chapter VII.

In no. 74 the keyboard instrument is *Tasto Solo* ; see the note on this movement, p. 51.

No. 58, which requires only three instruments, and those movements that employ only the strings of Orchestra II, can be used to give the other players a break, or left till the end of the rehearsal.

TABLE V

MOVEMENTS REQUIRING CHOIR II, BOTH ORCHESTRAS, AND SOLOISTS

25, 26	Tenor
33, up to letter C	Soprano and Contralto
36	Contralto
70	Contralto
77	All four soloists

Bach specified Choir II for these movements; but it is generally better to have them sung by both choirs.

TABLE VI

CHORUSES REQUIRING ONLY ONE ORCHESTRA

Orchestra I and Choir I	7, 14, 15, 71
Orchestra II and Choir II	45, 71

Chapter VII

THE INDIVIDUAL MOVEMENTS

IN THE FOLLOWING NOTES, the headings give Bach's own instructions for using the choirs and orchestras singly or together. Better results can sometimes be obtained by disregarding his instructions : see the notes on no. 25 and other movements.

The headings also give the authors' recommendations (not Bach's instructions ; see p. 13) for the allocation of the figured continuo to harpsichord or organ. In some movements both instruments are required ; confusion cannot arise if it is remembered that the harpsichord is recommended for accompanying the Evangelist and the minor characters (except in parts of nos 39, 50, 71, and 73, where special instructions are given), and the organ for all choruses.

The organ is also mentioned in all movements where the sayings of Jesus occur. Bach intended these passages to be accompanied by the organ as well as by Orchestra I ; but many conductors may prefer the simplicity of effect obtainable by using the strings alone. For no. 71 see p. 50.

The pauses in the chorales are simply conventional signs indicating the ends of the lines, like the double-bars in present-day hymnbooks. They often occur in the organ chorale preludes at points where actual pauses cannot be made. Therefore, although it is legitimate to hold all the pauses, it is equally legitimate, and much more satisfactory, to treat the chorales like ordinary hymns and observe the pauses only where the words admit of a break. All concerned must know exactly where breath is to be taken.

Bach no doubt intended his audiences to sing in the chorales ; but nowadays it is difficult to obtain satisfactory results in this way, and it is generally wise to have it clearly understood that the audience is not to sing at all. Its opportunities are in any case limited. Of the twelve chorales, only seven are reasonably well known in England : nos 16, 21, 23, 44, 53, 63, 72. Nos 21, 23, and 63 are too high for unison singing, which, moreover, would hardly be tolerable in no. 72. Thus, the only chorales that the audience can really sing are nos 16, 44, and 53.

If the audience is to sing, broad treatment is essential, and the organist must give plenty of support.

The nuances suggested below apply only when the chorales are to be sung by the choir alone. Even then, a certain breadth of treatment must be maintained ; to multiply nuances and emphasize individual words produces a most unsuitable effect of preciosity.

The vocal score (V.S.) referred to is the Elgar-Atkins (Novello) edition of 1938. During the preparation of this book a few misprints in the vocal score have been found and corrected. The most important of them are mentioned below.

Almost every watch gives 300 ticks to the minute. Metronomic accuracy can therefore be obtained, without using the instrument itself, at the following rates :

150 = 2 ticks
100 = 3 ticks
75 = 4 ticks
60 = 5 ticks
50 = 6 ticks

* * *

PART I

Duration about an hour and a half; with full Da Capos, some five minutes longer

I. CHORUS

Both choirs. Both orchestras. 6 mins to 9 mins 40 secs. Continuo : organ.

The timings imply metronomic rates between about ♩. = 60 and ♩. = 40 : a wide range, due largely, no doubt, to differences in the size of choirs and resonance of buildings. The beat must be felt as four in the bar, not twelve ; otherwise the chorus may drag.

Some conductors increase the pace slightly in the orchestral interlude just before letter D, returning to Tempo I at F. In the orchestral figuration that begins at D, the staccato should not be exaggerated.

According to Schweitzer, this chorus 'depicts a crowd moving excitedly about, crying aloud, roaring' : a conception that implies energetic treatment. But the chorus is also, and perhaps more generally, regarded as an introductory meditation ; in which case it is effective to begin *pp*, make a big diminuendo four bars before the end, and finish *ppp*.

The chorale beginning at B must ring out above all the other parts. Unless extra sopranos are available for this movement alone, it is probably best sung by half the sopranos of both choirs, so that there are twice as many singers on the chorale as on either of the other soprano parts. With support from the organ, as specified by Bach, this is sufficient.

The chorale is sometimes played by a trumpet. This would be helpful when there is no organ ; but otherwise should be avoided, since the trumpet has no place in Bach's Passiontide orchestra.

The interjections by Choir II ('Whom? How?') should be well sustained.

2. RECITATIVE

EVANGELIST AND JESUS. Orchestra I. 1 min. Continuo : harpsichord and organ.

A diminuendo in the last two bars is effective. It can be prepared for by a slight crescendo in the previous bar.

Bar 3 clearly will not do as it stands ; Schneider may be right in making the string basses and organ enter on the third crotchet, not the second.

3. CHORALE

Both choirs. Both orchestras. 1 min to 1 min 25 secs. Continuo : organ.

It is effective to make a diminuendo in the third line of words, with the last line *pp*. The quietness can be emphasized by omitting the woodwind and organ ; the harmony notes thus lost are not important.

4. RECITATIVE

EVANGELIST. 25 secs. Continuo : harpsichord.

Sir Hugh Allen was perhaps the first to omit the final chord of C and run this recitative on into no. 5, in an attempt to secure the continuity required by the words. It is rather doubtful whether one really gains anything by following his example, the dramatic fitness of no. 5 being questionable ; moreover, a glance at the rest of the Passion will show that Bach was perfectly capable of running a recitative on when he wanted to. If there is a failure of imagination here, it goes too deep to be mended so simply. See the note on no. 5.

5. CHORUS

Both choirs. Both orchestras. 12 secs. Continuo : organ.

Attempts to suggest 'subtilty' by beginning this chorus *p*, with a crescendo, are not altogether successful ; it is difficult to make an eight-part chorus in C major sound like the subdued voices of a few conspiratorial high officials. Perhaps Bach's imagination failed him here ; he may well have been not greatly interested in these introductory passages of narrative. It may be better to take this chorus at its face value than to try to give it a dramatic significance that does not seem to be in it.

6. RECITATIVE

EVANGELIST. 35 secs. Continuo : harpsichord.

7. CHORUS

Choir I. Orchestra I. 30 secs. Continuo : organ.

Choir I is large enough to express the indignation of a few disciples. The tenors should not be allowed to make too much of their A flat in bar 6.

8. RECITATIVE

EVANGELIST AND JESUS. Orchestra I. 1 min 50 secs. Continuo : harpsichord and organ.

Bars 10–11 may well be quieter and slower, if that suits the soloist.

9. ACCOMPANIED RECITATIVE

Contralto Solo. Orchestra I. 1 min 5 secs to 1 min 30 secs. Continuo : organ, with one cello and one bass.

The organist may play detached chords for manuals only, as indicated in the part. Alternatively, he may provide a continuous background by sustaining the upper notes of each chord, with or without doubling the bass in full-length crotchets on a very soft pedal stop. This sustained treatment is suggested by Bach's figuring in bars 3, 6, 8, and 9.

A soloist with good breath-control will like this as slow as ♪ = 56.

10. ARIA

Contralto Solo. Orchestra I. 2 mins 50 secs, if the return is made to letter C ; 4 mins 25 secs, or more, with a full Da Capo. Continuo : harpsichord, with one cello.

11. RECITATIVE

EVANGELIST AND JUDAS. 50 secs. Continuo : harpsichord.

12. ARIA

Soprano Solo. Orchestra II. With full Da Capo, 4 mins 20 secs to 5 mins 30 secs. Continuo : harpsichord.

Schweitzer says this should not be too slow ; a vague expression, which probably comes to the same thing as saying that it should not be faster than ♩ = 60.

Here, as in other movements, the vocal score gives only a skeleton realization of the continuo, which the player should thicken up. Conductors who prefer to use the organ should remember that its part also is probably not full enough.

13. RECITATIVE

EVANGELIST. 15 secs. Continuo : harpsichord.

14. CHORUS

Choir I. Orchestra I. 23 secs. Continuo : organ.

A small group of disciples is asking a question of no great importance. This chorus need not be louder than *mf* ; not, at any rate, to begin with.

15. RECITATIVE AND CHORUS

EVANGELIST AND JESUS. Choir I. Orchestra I. 2 mins 7 secs to 2 mins 15 secs. Continuo : harpsichord and organ.

The *Allegro* at the chorus 'Lord, is it I ?' is Bach's own mark. It would be easier to observe with the German words, which have only three syllables (*Herr, bin ich's ?*).

This question should be tentative and quiet, but with a crescendo to suggest growing excitement. Choir I is large enough.

16. CHORALE

Both choirs. Both orchestras. 1 min 5 secs to 1 min 20 secs. Continuo : organ.

This is the answer of Humanity to the disciples' question. As there can be no doubt about our guilt, *forte* seems at least as suitable as the *piano* suggested by Elgar and Atkins.

17. RECITATIVE

EVANGELIST, JESUS, AND JUDAS. Orchestra I. 4 mins to 4 mins 35 secs. Continuo : harpsichord and organ.

The *p*'s (Bach's marks) may well be interpreted as *pp*'s, with a rise to *mf* for the inspiring vision of the last few bars.

18. ACCOMPANIED RECITATIVE

Soprano Solo. Orchestra I. 1 min 40 secs to 2 mins 30 secs. The latter timing implies a metronomic rate slower than ♪ = 50. Continuo : organ, with full basses.

The organist should fill in certain notes that are implied by the figuring, but not given in the organ part : e.g., the G sharp in the second half of bar 2, and the thirds in the last two bars.

As in all such passages, the basses must play expressively, with a slight stress on the first of each pair of quavers.

19. ARIA

Soprano Solo. Orchestra I. 3 mins 15 secs to 4 mins. Continuo : harpsichord, with one cello and one bass.

One can shorten the Da Capo by returning to C ; but there seems little point in doing so.

20. RECITATIVE

EVANGELIST AND JESUS. Orchestra I. 1 min 30 secs. Continuo : harpsichord and organ.

The tempo and dynamic marks are authentic. It is perhaps best to lead into the *Moderato* by making a rallentando in the first half of bar 10 ; but an abrupt change is easier to manage.

In bar 9, the eighth semiquaver of Violin II is given as B both in the original score and parts, and in the B.G. edition. As the B.G. editor pointed out, it should clearly be C sharp. The emendation has been made in the Novello vocal score and violin part.

21. CHORALE

Both choirs. Both orchestras. 1 min 22 secs. Continuo : organ.

22. RECITATIVE

EVANGELIST, PETER, AND JESUS. Orchestra I. 1 min 8 secs. Continuo : harpsichord and organ.

23. CHORALE

Both choirs. Both orchestras. 1 min 28 secs. Continuo : organ.

It is effective to make a slight diminuendo during the third line of words, take the fourth line *mp*, and swell out again in the penultimate line.

24. RECITATIVE

EVANGELIST AND JESUS. Orchestra I. 2 mins 12 secs to 2 mins 40 secs. Continuo : harpsichord and organ.

Bar 7 may be played *pp espressivo*. A good 32-foot pedal stop can be used with great effect from the second half of bar 12 to the end.

25. ACCOMPANIED RECITATIVE WITH CHORALE

Tenor Solo. Choir II. Both orchestras (full basses of Orchestra I). 3 mins 30 secs. Continuo : organ.

In this movement Bach used recorders, not flutes, in Orchestra I.

The continuo of Orchestra I is marked *pianissimo*, in full. According to Schneider, this means *ppp*. Bach perhaps found that his violonists ignored any less extreme mark ; the other instruments are marked *p*. However, his dynamic marks often do not bear their normal modern meaning, and there is justification for a warmer treatment than is suggested by *p*. A highly effective contrast can then be obtained by singing the chorale *pp* : unaccompanied, except by the cellos and basses, to leave the vocal tone clear and pure. Good *pp* tone is easier to obtain if both choirs sing.

In bars 18, 21, and 22, certain harmony notes, implied by the figuring, are omitted from the Elgar-Atkins organ part. The organist can supply them unobtrusively without spoiling the general unaccompanied effect.

26. ARIA AND CHORUS

Tenor Solo. Choir II. Both orchestras. 6 mins to 6 mins 30 secs. Continuo : with the choir, organ : with the soloist, one cello and harpsichord. The tenor and cello parts occasionally cross, but not in such a way that the progression of the bass is obscured by the omission of sixteen-foot tone.

The choral passages should be *pp* throughout, with *ppp* at the end. As in no. 25, they should be sung by both choirs.

The first chord in the last bar but one, V.S. p. 53, is C minor ; not C major, as in some issues of the V.S. The E does not become natural until the third beat.

27. RECITATIVE

EVANGELIST AND JESUS. Orchestra I. 1 min 8 secs. Continuo : harpsichord and organ.

28. ACCOMPANIED RECITATIVE

Bass Solo. Orchestra II. 1 min 25 secs. Continuo : organ.

29. ARIA

Bass Solo. Orchestra II. 3 mins 50 secs to 4 mins 10 secs. Continuo : organ.

This aria must not be allowed to drag; ♪ = 130 is not too fast. Even so, with a full Da Capo it is very long ; and on the whole it is better to return to C, the organist beginning with a plain chord of C minor instead of a 9–8 suspension.

30. RECITATIVE

EVANGELIST AND JESUS. Orchestra I. 1 min 44 secs. Continuo : harpsichord and organ.

31. CHORALE

Both choirs. Both orchestras. 1 min 40 secs. Continuo : organ.

In the last line, on the word 'peace', the alto note is B—not G, as in some issues of the V.S.

32. RECITATIVE

EVANGELIST, JESUS, AND JUDAS. Orchestra I. 2 mins 53 secs. Continuo : harpsichord and organ.

33. DUET AND CHORUS

Soprano and Contralto Solos. Both choirs. Both orchestras. 5 mins 14 secs to 6 mins 47 secs.

Up to letter C, a keyboard instrument is specified only with the choir, and is hardly worth using at all. For the first sixteen bars after C, the voices are accompanied only by the organ and the string basses. The organ must be used in bars 2–5 after C ; but after that the effect is often clearer without it. The organist should keep his reeds in reserve for a powerful entry at F.

The *Andante* at the beginning is authentic, though found only in the Flute II part. The *un poco piano*, also authentic, applies only to the strings of Orchestra I ; subsequent marks show that the flutes and oboes begin *f* as usual. No doubt Bach's intention was to prevent them from being drowned by the strings, which are in unison.

The choral ejaculations during the Duet are written for Choir II, but are best sung by both choirs. Here Bach marked the orchestral parts staccato. The vocal parts need not necessarily be staccato also, and a great increase of power can be obtained by keeping the first syllables broad, with the consonants uttered before the beat and the vowels of 'loose' and 'leave' pressed firmly. The same applies to the fugal exposition at letter C, and especially to the first syllables of 'lightnings' and 'thunders', where all choirs have a strong tendency to sing staccato.

34. RECITATIVE

EVANGELIST AND JESUS. Orchestra I. 2 mins 45 secs. Continuo : harpsichord and organ.

35. CHORUS

Both choirs (in four parts only). Both orchestras. 8 mins. Continuo : organ.

The small notes in the vocal score represent obbligato parts, and are effective when the choir is being accompanied by piano alone. They have nothing to do with the continuo, which at these points is *Tasto Solo*.

As in no. 1, Bach meant the organist to support the chorale melody.

The slurred two-note figures of the orchestral parts must be phrased sharply throughout. The vocal shakes should be sung ; the figuration is so obviously designed for them that it sounds pointless if they are omitted. They are not as difficult as they look, since they can be sung quite slowly.

The tempo is determined by the chorale, and must be fast enough for each line to be felt as a unit ; ♩ = 50 is a usual rate.

When studying this chorus, it is helpful to read Parry's fine description of it (*Johann Sebastian Bach*, p. 270). Easy as its notes are, there is no movement in the Passion that makes greater demands on the musicianship of the singers ; intense concentration is required to maintain unity and make the growth of this monumental movement out of a simple hymn-tune sound inevitable.

This chorus was an afterthought ; Part I originally ended with a plain chorale, which has been included as an Appendix (no. 35A) in the latest issues of the V.S., and may well be used by choirs who find no. 35 beyond their powers. It takes about 1 min 15 secs, and requires both choirs and orchestras, with the organ as the continuo instrument.

PART II

Duration just under two hours; with full Da Capos, five or ten minutes longer

36. ARIA AND CHORUS

Contralto Solo. Choir II. Both orchestras. 4 mins 20 secs to 4 mins 40 secs. Continuo: harpsichord with the soloist, organ with the choir.

The organist should play according to the figuring, not simply double the voices. For instance, a firm full chord of D is essential at letter B.

Both choirs should sing; and for the choral passages *p legato* is perhaps more appropriate than the Elgar-Atkins *mf*. As in no. 35, the vocal shakes should be sung.

A flute and an oboe d'amore play in unison with the first violins of Orchestra I. The part is troublesome, owing to its large compass: the low A is too low for flute and ordinary oboe, the high D impossible for cor anglais and very difficult for the oboe d'amore itself. There are precedents in Bach's scores for playing impossibly low notes an octave higher; but in this movement it is probably best to omit them altogether, the flute and ordinary oboe simply playing as many notes as they can.

37. RECITATIVE

EVANGELIST. 1 min 10 secs. Continuo: harpsichord.

38. CHORALE

Both choirs. Both orchestras. 1 min 10 secs. Continuo : organ.

39. RECITATIVE

EVANGELIST, TWO FALSE WITNESSES, AND HIGH PRIEST. Orchestra II. 1 min 15 secs.

String basses and organ make a suitable accompaniment for the ponderous insincerity of the False Witnesses. The harpsichord should be used for the rest of the movement.

40. ACCOMPANIED RECITATIVE

Tenor Solo. Orchestra II. 1 min 20 secs. Continuo : harpsichord.

The B.G. editor did not know that Bach himself wrote out a viola da gamba part for this movement, and that there is therefore good authority for the version relegated to the Appendix of that edition.

The quaver chords for the oboes should be given their full length. They must be backed up by the harpsichord, particularly if the viola da gamba part is for any reason not used. The figuring of bars 2 and 3 suggests sustained chords ; conductors may like to try the effect of using the organ as well.

41. ARIA

Tenor Solo. Orchestra II. 3 mins 18 secs to 3 mins 40 secs. Continuo : harpsichord, with one cello or viola da gamba.

The tenor and string bass parts occasionally cross ; but, as in no. 26, there is no need for sixteen-foot tone. The cello and viola da gamba parts are identical ;

Schneider seems to think that Bach preferred the latter.

42. RECITATIVE AND CHORUS

EVANGELIST, HIGH PRIEST, AND JESUS. Both choirs. Both orchestras. 1 min 53 secs. Continuo : harpsichord and organ.

Here, and here only, the 1911 translation ('He guilty is of death') is perhaps preferable to that of 1938 ('He is worthy of death'). It is given in Appendix I, for the convenience of conductors who cannot obtain a copy of the 1911 edition.

43. RECITATIVE AND CHORUS

EVANGELIST. Both choirs. Both orchestras. 37 secs. Continuo : harpsichord and organ.

This chorus gains effect from a rather heavy start, with an accelerando.

44. CHORALE

Both choirs. Both orchestras. 1 min 26 secs. Continuo : organ.

The world at large replies to the taunts of a local crowd ; this should surely be sung at a determined *forte*. Compare no. 16.

45. RECITATIVE AND CHORUS

EVANGELIST, TWO MAIDS, AND PETER. Choir II. Orchestra II. 1 min 18 secs. Continuo : harpsichord and organ.

Choir II is strong enough for this casual remark by the bystanders.

46. RECITATIVE

EVANGELIST AND PETER. 1 min 30 secs. Continuo : harpsichord.

An unusually long break is appropriate after this recitative, and helps to prepare for no. 47, one of the finest arias in the work.

47. ARIA

Contralto Solo. Orchestra I. 6 mins 30 secs to 7 mins 30 secs : a considerable range of tempo. It takes good breath-control to make this aria effective at ♪ = 88 or any slower tempo. Continuo : organ.

In the Autograph Score the string basses play *arco* at times ; but in the original parts they are *pizzicato* throughout. Conductors may like to try the effect of letting the organist sustain the outline of the bass on soft pedal stops.

There is no authority for muting the *tutti* strings. All the performers should be warned to listen to each other, to secure unanimity ; and the ornaments, to which the melodic lines owe much of their expressiveness, must on no account be omitted.

48. CHORALE

Both choirs. Both orchestras. 1 min 50 secs. Continuo : organ.

The Elgar-Atkins *p* may well be changed to *pp*, and the accompaniment lightened by omitting the woodwind, or even the organ as well.

The first chord of this chorale is as in Ex. 4, and the first chord of the third line of words is as in Ex. 5. Some editions wrongly begin both lines in the same way (like line 1).

The second alto note in bar 4 is F sharp ; not G sharp, as in some issues of the V.S. Compare bar 8.

49. RECITATIVE AND CHORUS

EVANGELIST AND JUDAS. Both choirs. Both orchestras. 1 min 30 secs. Continuo : harpsichord and organ.

The chorus may begin slowly and heavily, with a crescendo and accelerando. The 1938 translation is a great improvement.

50. RECITATIVE

EVANGELIST AND TWO PRIESTS. Orchestra I. 50 secs. Continuo : harpsichord with the Evangelist : organ and string basses with the Two Priests.

51. ARIA

Bass Solo. Orchestra II. 3 mins 45 secs. Continuo : harpsichord.

52. RECITATIVE

EVANGELIST, PILATE, AND JESUS. Orchestra I. 1 min 25 secs. Continuo : harpsichord and organ.

53. CHORALE

Both choirs. Both orchestras. 1 min 26 secs. Continuo : organ.

54. RECITATIVE AND CHORUSES

EVANGELIST, PILATE, AND PILATE'S WIFE. Both choirs (four-part in 'Let Him be crucified'). Both orchestras. 2 mins 50 secs. Continuo : harpsichord and organ.

The crowd cannot really have answered Pilate in a single unanimous shout of 'Barabbas!' ; and at the first glance one might think that Bach's dramatic imagination failed him here (cf. no. 5). But this is something better than mere realism : Bach imagined the crowd as so intent on the death of Jesus that Pilate's question acted on them like pulling a trigger. No doubt his conception was influenced by his having to write a chorus on one word —three syllables, the first accented. In English it is the second syllable that takes the accent ; and this leads to a difference of opinion. Some conductors, acting on the generally accepted principle that Bach's notes should be adjusted to suit the words of the English Bible, call for a strong accent on the semiquaver, or go so far as to rewrite the passage somewhat thus :

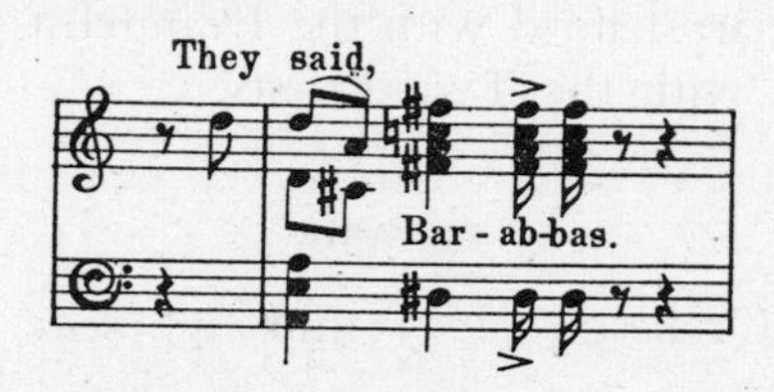

Others argue that since there is no change of chord during the word 'Barabbas', any accent achieved in this way is obviously artificial ; they hold that the true effect can only be obtained by leaving the passage as Bach wrote it, with the first syllable stressed. This is a matter that one must think out for oneself.

Two bars after the 'Barabbas' passage, Pilate's first note is E, not D.

55. CHORALE

Both choirs. Both orchestras. 1 min 20 secs. Continuo : organ.

56. RECITATIVE

EVANGELIST AND PILATE. 10 secs. Continuo : harpsichord.

57. ACCOMPANIED RECITATIVE

Soprano Solo. Orchestra I. 1 min 45 secs to 2 mins. Continuo : organ, with full string basses.

58. ARIA

Soprano Solo. Orchestra I. 5 mins 10 secs to 6 mins 52 secs. No continuo.

The singer and the three woodwind players must each be intimately acquainted with all four parts, and the treatment of the pauses must be clearly understood.

59. RECITATIVE AND CHORUSES

EVANGELIST AND PILATE. Both choirs (four-part). Both orchestras. 2 mins 31 secs. Continuo : harpsichord and organ.

60. ACCOMPANIED RECITATIVE

Contralto Solo. Orchestra II. 1 min 30 secs to 1 min 50 secs. Continuo : organ.

If the singer begins with a powerful cry, some dynamic changes will be required. They should be agreed on beforehand and marked in the string parts. According to Schneider, Bach himself marked the upper strings *p*; but this may mean only that he did not wish the voice to be drowned. There is, in any case, no doubt that the string figuration was suggested by the action of scourging and should be played with some energy.

For the first viola note of bar 10, Schneider prints C sharp instead of the B.G.'s illogical D. The Autograph Score is not clear.

61. ARIA

Contralto Solo. Orchestra II. 4 mins 39 secs to 5 mins, with the Da Capo shortened by returning to one bar after letter C. The full Da Capo would take about another minute and a half. Continuo : harpsichord.

The ornaments in bars 10–11, etc., are ordinary *Vorschläge* : ♪, not ♪. See the Autograph Score.

62. RECITATIVE AND CHORUS

EVANGELIST. Both choirs. Both orchestras. 1 min 15 secs. Continuo : harpsichord and organ.

63. CHORALE

Both choirs. Both orchestras. 3 mins to 3 mins 33 secs. Continuo : organ.

Both verses of this chorale should be sung : the second may be *pp*, accompanied perhaps by strings only.

64. RECITATIVE

EVANGELIST. 1 min. Continuo : harpsichord.

65. ACCOMPANIED RECITATIVE

Bass Solo. Orchestra I. 47 secs to 1 min. Continuo : organ, with one or two cellos and one bass.

A cello adaptation of the viola da gamba part is generally played, but a special part can be obtained for use when the proper instrument is available.

66. ARIA

Bass Solo. Orchestra I. 6 mins 13 secs to 6 mins 45 secs. Continuo : harpsichord, with one or two cellos and one bass. For the viola da gamba obbligato, see no. 65.

67. RECITATIVE AND CHORUSES

EVANGELIST. Both choirs (partly in four parts). Both orchestras. 3 mins 40 secs. Continuo : harpsichord and organ.

It is effective to begin the second chorus rather slowly, and work it up, with an allargando at the end. It is very doubtful how the continuo part should be treated in bars 3 and 4 of this chorus, and during the final unison passage. Conductors should consult Arnold (see Appendix IV) pp. 415-7, and decide for themselves.

68. RECITATIVE

EVANGELIST. 10 secs. Continuo : harpsichord.

69. ACCOMPANIED RECITATIVE

Contralto Solo. Orchestra I. 1 min 50 secs to 2 mins 10 secs. Continuo : organ, with full string basses.

This movement, like no. 60, will stand varied treatment by the soloist. A *pp* close seems most suitable.

70. ARIA AND CHORUS

Contralto Solo. Choir II. Both orchestras. 4 mins 9 secs. Continuo : with the soloist, harpsichord, two cellos, and one bass : with the choir, organ.

In the choral interjections Bach marked the quavers staccato ; but his dots are often best interpreted as stress dashes, and these chords should all be kept fairly broad.

In some issues of the V.S. there is a *p* in bar 1 ; it is not Bach's mark.

71. RECITATIVE AND CHORUSES

EVANGELIST AND JESUS. Choirs I and II singly. Orchestra I with the soloists and Choir I: Orchestra II with Choir II. 2 mins 42 secs to 3 mins 10 secs. Continuo : harpsichord and organ.

The organist accompanies the Evangelist's 'My God, my God, why hast Thou forsaken Me?' as well as the Jesus and the choirs. A good 32-foot stop will be effective in both the 'Eli' passages. The *Adagio* in bar 7 is Bach's mark.

The onlookers' comments are rather casual, and can suitably be sung by Choirs I and II singly, as indicated by Bach. A long silence is appropriate after 'Let us see whether Elias will come to save Him'.

72. CHORALE

Both choirs. 2 mins 5 secs.

This chorale, the central point of the work and the kernel of our faith, requires exceptional treatment. In present-day conditions, a thick congregational accompaniment is not to be thought of ; and as it fortunately happens that the organ contributes nothing very significant, the choir should sing unaccompanied and *pp*, very simply but with intense feeling. The basses should divide to take the low E's of the string part.

73. RECITATIVE AND CHORUS

EVANGELIST. Both choirs (in four parts only). Orchestra I with the Evangelist : both orchestras with the choirs. 3 mins 25 secs. Continuo : bars 1–10, organ with full string basses : 11–18, harpsichord : 18–21, organ : 21–end, harpsichord.

Sung rhythmically in strict time, the effect of the first ten bars is overwhelming. In bars 1–4 the organist should be liberal with staccatos ; in bars 5–7 he may make a big crescendo (by opening the Swell box) during the first half of each bar, and a diminuendo in the second half to avoid obliterating the soloist. For bars 8 and 9, a long diminuendo and rallentando is appropriate. On some organs these effects may be rather troublesome to get. If the organist is not thoroughly familiar with his instrument already, he should be given opportunities for practice before the rehearsal with the singer.

The chorus cannot be too slow or too smooth. Beginning and ending *pp*, it should rise in the middle to an exaltation matching the message it conveys.

74. ACCOMPANIED RECITATIVE

Bass Solo. Orchestra I. 2 mins 40 secs.

When he wrote the Score, Bach seems to have meant a keyboard instrument to be used in the normal way ; but the original figured continuo part is *Tasto Solo*. This should mean that the double-basses are silent, and the organist does not play chords—only the bass part, at eight-foot pitch ; but the movement seems to call for depth, and this the organist can supply by using a soft pedal stop, with a 32-foot here and there.

75. ARIA

Bass Solo. Orchestra I. 5 mins 37 secs, if the Dal Segno is shortened by returning to the fourth or fifth bar after letter C. A full Dal Segno would take nearly two minutes more.

When the shortened version is used, the singer should

hold a high B flat (as in bar 10) as if he were singing the aria in full.

Continuo : harpsichord.

If the long continuance of oboe da caccia (cor anglais) tone is found wearisome, these instruments can be omitted during the middle section of the aria.

76. RECITATIVE AND CHORUS

EVANGELIST AND PILATE. Both choirs (mainly in four parts). Both orchestras. 2 mins 37 secs. Continuo : harpsichord and organ.

77. ACCOMPANIED RECITATIVE WITH CHORUS

Solo Quartet. Choir II. Both orchestras. 3 mins 22 secs. Continuo : organ.

In this movement the means of expression are so diverse, with all four soloists alternating with the choir, that there is some risk of its sounding disjointed. Rhythmical unity must therefore be maintained at all costs ; only the slightest deviations from strict time can be tolerated.

According to Schneider, Bach marked the choir *p* (not *pp*, as in the V.S.), but the latter is more likely to give present-day singers the right impression. Good tone is easier to obtain if both choirs sing. The quietness of the close can be emphasized by making the third choral passage slightly louder.

78. CHORUS

Both choirs. Both orchestras. 7 mins 45 secs to 9 mins. Continuo : organ.

This overwhelming close lends itself to widely differing treatments. The slower of the timings quoted above implies a metronomic rate slower than ♩ = 50 ; but this is only possible with large forces, and there is no harm in taking the chorus considerably faster. The pace must not change at all.

Most of the *f*'s, as well as the *p*'s and *pp*'s, are Bach's own marks ; but, as usual, it is unnecessary to take them literally. It is probably best to reach a *f* (in the present-day sense) only here and there, the general dynamic level being nearer *p*, with *pp* at the end and between letters F and G. The latter passage needs special attention ; once more, really intense *pp* tone is easier to obtain if both choirs sing.

Chapter VIII

PROGRAMME NOTES

FULL INFORMATION must be given if audiences are to understand the Passion. At a complete performance it is best to sell the book of words, which can be obtained from Messrs Novello. There are two forms of it: one giving only the words, the other including the music of the chorales. The soloists' names, with other information about the performance, can be printed on a cover ; the book of words can then be sewn inside.

If this is too ambitious, one can distribute a synopsis ; a specimen is given below. Conductors may wish to reprint this as it stands ; if so, they must obtain permission to do so from Messrs Novello. Those who prefer to write programme notes for themselves should note that they also must obtain permission if they wish to quote the words of the English translation.

The programme notes should give the audience clear instructions to sing in certain chorales, or not at all, as the case may be. See p. 30.

* * *

IN the Protestant Church of Germany it is still the custom, as it was long before Bach's day, to hold services during Holy Week at which the Gospel narrative of the Passion is read, punctuated by hymns in which the congregation joins.

Services of this kind were found to lend themselves to elaboration, and developed naturally into musical settings of the Passion. Of these the greatest is the Passion according to St Matthew by Johann Sebastian Bach, which is being performed today.

The narrative, instead of being read, is sung in recitative by a tenor, who represents the Evangelist. A bass sings the words of Jesus ; other soloists take the minor characters, such as Peter and Judas. The Jesus is distinguished from the Evangelist and the minor characters by being accompanied by strings, instead of a harpsichord or piano. Words spoken by the disciples in a body, or shouted by the mob, are set as choruses.

At the original services the hymns, whose words and tunes were well known, were sung by the congregation. They could thus be made to serve as comments on the main incidents of the narrative—as a rule, such comments as apply to, or might be made by, the Church at large. The hymns used by Bach in the Passion were meant to be sung in the same way, and to serve the same purpose. Further comment, usually of a more personal kind, is provided by a quartet of soloists singing accompanied recitatives and arias.

Finally, there are four great choruses that serve to introduce and to sum up the two Parts into which the work is divided.

Listening to music is not a matter of sitting in a state of passive receptivity ; it is an action, and requires conscious effort. All music, therefore, requires a sympathetic and co-operative audience ; and this is particularly true of a work like the Passion, which was meant to be performed at a church service, not at a concert.

It is hoped that the following notes will help the audience to co-operate. They give the drift of the words, movement by movement, and draw attention to a few points whose significance, obvious to an eighteenth-century German congregation, might be obscure to an English concert audience of today.

PART I

1. CHORUS. 'Come, ye daughters, share my mourning': an invitation to listen to the story of the Passion and consider its significance. The two choirs sing question and answer, thus:

Choir I: See Him,
Choir II: Whom?
Choir I: The Bridegroom Christ. See Him,
Choir II: How?
Choir I: A spotless Lamb.

As a comment, a separate body of sopranos sings the first verse of the Passiontide hymn 'O Lamb of God most holy'. The familiar hymn, with all its associations, must have had a great emotional effect in Bach's day. Unfortunately it has no associations for English audiences, who can do no more than try, by an intellectual effort, to understand and sympathize with Bach's intentions.

2. RECITATIVE. Jesus says to His disciples, 'Ye know that after two days is the Passover, and the Son of Man shall be delivered over to be crucified.'

3. HYMN. 'O blessed Jesu, how hast Thou offended?' The world asks how its Saviour can deserve such a punishment.

4. RECITATIVE. The Evangelist tells how the rulers conspire to kill Jesus, but

5. CHORUS. 'Not upon the feast, lest haply there be an uproar among the people.'

6. RECITATIVE. At Bethany, a woman pours precious ointment over her Lord. The disciples protest:

7. CHORUS. 'To what purpose is this waste?'

8. RECITATIVE. Jesus reproves the disciples, and foretells His death.

9, 10. CONTRALTO SOLOS. Meditations on the woman's symbolic preparation for Jesus' death.

11. RECITATIVE. Judas goes to the Chief Priests and bargains for his thirty pieces of silver.

12. SOPRANO SOLO. The soloist comments on the betrayal.

13. RECITATIVE. The disciples come to Jesus, asking :

14. CHORUS. 'Where wilt Thou that we prepare for Thee to eat the Passover ?'

15. RECITATIVE AND CHORUS. He sends them to arrange for the room. As they eat, He says, 'Verily I say to you, that one of you shall betray Me.' The disciples anxiously ask, 'Lord, is it I ?'

16. HYMN. ' 'Tis I whose sin now binds Thee'. It is the world speaking.

17. RECITATIVE. Jesus points to Judas as His betrayer. He blesses the Bread and Wine.

18, 19. SOPRANO SOLOS. Meditations : 'His Flesh and Blood, O precious gift ! He leaves us for our souls' refreshment.' 'Jesus, Saviour, I am Thine, Come and dwell my heart within.'

20. RECITATIVE. They go to the Mount of Olives. Jesus quotes the prophecy : 'I will smite the Shepherd, and the sheep of the flock shall be scattered abroad.'

21. HYMN. 'Receive me, my Redeemer, My Shepherd, make me Thine.'

22. RECITATIVE. Jesus foretells Peter's denial.

23. HYMN. The world speaks, with the disciples : 'Here would I stand beside Thee.'

24. RECITATIVE. They go to Gethsemane. Jesus says, 'My soul is exceeding sorrowful, even unto death : tarry ye here, and watch with Me.'

25, 26. TENOR SOLOS WITH CHORUS. A commentary on no. 24. In no. 25, the tenor enlarges on Jesus' sorrow : 'O grief ! that bows the Saviour's troubled heart!', and the choir replies, 'My Saviour, why must all this ill befall Thee? . . . God took the debt from me . . . On Thee He laid it.' In no. 26 the tenor continues, 'I would beside my Lord be watching', and the choir adds, 'And so our sin will fall asleep.'

27. RECITATIVE. Jesus prays, 'Let this cup pass from Me.'

28, 29. BASS SOLOS. The soloist looks on, longing to share his Lord's burden.

30. RECITATIVE. Jesus finds the disciples asleep, tells Peter to 'Watch and pray', and Himself prays again : 'If this cup may not pass away from Me, except I drink it, Thy will be done.'

31. HYMN. 'O Father, let Thy will be done.'

32. RECITATIVE. Judas arrives ; Jesus is arrested.

33. DUET WITH CHORUS. As the procession moves along two women cry, 'Behold, my Saviour now is taken.' The choir breaks in three times, 'Loose Him! leave Him! bind Him not!', and then cries, 'Have lightnings and thunders their fury forgotten?' There is a dramatic silence, followed by 'Then open, O fathomless pit, all thy terrors! Destroy them. . . . The treach'rous betrayer, the merciless throng.'

34. RECITATIVE. Jesus stays the hand of one who would defend Him, and the disciples forsake Him.

35. CHORUS. 'O man, thy grievous sin bemoan, For which Christ left His Father's throne, . . . The shameful Cross enduring.' The world bewails the frailty of man, typified by the disciples' desertion. The sopranos sing the first verse of what was in Bach's day a familiar Passiontide hymn, one line at a time (there are twelve lines). The other voices provide a slightly elaborated accompaniment. The orchestra supplies an introduction, conclusion, and interludes between the lines, holding the whole magnificent movement together by its concentration on a single independent theme.

PART II

36. CONTRALTO SOLO WITH CHORUS. The soloist seeks her Saviour : 'Ah! now is my Saviour gone.' The choir asks, 'Whither is thy beloved gone ? For we would go with thee to seek Him.'

37. RECITATIVE. Jesus is led before Caiaphas the High Priest, and the council seek false witnesses.

38. HYMN. 'How falsely doth the world accuse!'

39. RECITATIVE. Two false witnesses accuse Jesus. He does not answer them.

40, 41. TENOR SOLOS. The soloist praises patient endurance in affliction.

42. RECITATIVE AND CHORUS. The High Priest questions Jesus, and accuses Him of blasphemy. The crowd shouts, 'He guilty is of death.'

43. RECITATIVE AND CHORUS. They spit on Him and buffet Him, saying, 'Now tell us, Thou Christ, who is he that smote Thee?'

44. HYMN. The world replies, 'O Lord, who dares to smite Thee?'

45. RECITATIVE AND CHORUS. Peter is sitting outside ; he is accused by two maids and other bystanders.

46. RECITATIVE. Peter denies his Lord. The cock crows; he goes out and weeps bitterly.

47. CONTRALTO SOLO. The soloist voices our sympathy : 'Have mercy, Lord, on me, Regard my bitter weeping.'

48. HYMN. A hymn of trust and hope concludes the scene.

49. RECITATIVE AND CHORUS. Jesus is led before Pilate. Judas repents, and returns the thirty pieces of silver. The Elders say, 'But what is that to us ? see thou to that.'

50. RECITATIVE. Judas hangs himself. Two priests raise a quibble : 'It is the price of blood.'

51. BASS SOLO. 'Give me back my Lord.' The money having been returned, the soloist appeals to the priests.

52. RECITATIVE. The priests buy the potter's field. Pilate questions Jesus, and marvels at his silence.

53. HYMN. 'Commit thy way to Jesus, . . . He all thy sorrow shares.'

54. RECITATIVE AND CHORUSES. Pilate offers to release a prisoner. In a unanimous howl, the crowd chooses Barabbas. As for Jesus, 'Let Him be crucified!'

55. HYMN. 'O wondrous love . . . The Shepherd dying for his flock's protection.'

56. RECITATIVE. Pilate asks, 'Why, what evil hath He done ?'

57, 58. SOPRANO SOLOS. The soloist replies, 'To all men Jesus good hath done.' 'For love my Saviour now is dying.'

59. RECITATIVE AND CHORUSES. The crowd shouts ouder, 'Let Him be crucified!'; and, when Pilate washes his hands of the matter, 'His blood be on us and on our children.' Jesus is scourged.

60, 61. CONTRALTO SOLOS. The soloist protests, 'Tormentors, stay your hands !' 'If my tears be unavailing, Take the very heart of me.'

62. RECITATIVE AND CHORUS. Jesus is clothed in a scarlet robe, with a crown of thorns. The soldiers mock Him : Hail, hail, King of the Jews.'

63. HYMN. Two verses : 'O Sacred Head, surrounded By crown of piercing thorn' : 'In this Thy bitter Passion, Good Shepherd, think of me.'

64. RECITATIVE. Jesus is led away ; Simon of Cyrene bears the cross.

65, 66. BASS SOLOS. 'Come, healing Cross, O joy to share it ! My Saviour, lay on me its weight.'

67. Recitative and Choruses. The procession reaches Golgotha, and the crucifixion takes place. The passers-by say, 'Thou that destroyest the temple of God, and buildest it in three days, save Thyself.' The Chief Priest and the Scribes say, 'If He be King of Israel, let Him now come down from the cross, and we will believe Him.'

68. Recitative. The thieves cast the same in His teeth.

69. Contralto Solo. 'Ah, Golgotha! Unhappy Golgotha! The Lord of Glory here 'mid shame and scorn must perish.'

70. Contralto Solo with Chorus. The soloist sings, 'See the Saviour's outstretched hands! He would draw us to Himself. Come!' The choir ask, 'Come where?', and the soloist replies, 'In Jesu's bosom seek redemption.'

71. Recitative and Choruses. Jesus cries, 'Eli, Eli'. The crowd speculates, 'He calleth for Elias; let us see whether Elias will come to save Him.' There is silence. Jesus dies.

72. Hymn. The hymn speaks for each one of us: 'Be near me, Lord, when dying, O part not Thou from me.'

73. Recitative and Chorus. The Evangelist describes the portents that followed the Crucifixion. The choir sing, 'Truly this was the Son of God', here representing the whole Christian world as well as the centurion and bystanders. In the evening Joseph begs the Body.

74. Bass Solo. The soloist meditates on great events that have taken place in the evening.

75. Bass Solo. 'Make thee clean, my heart, from sin, Unto Jesus give thou welcome.'

76. Recitative and Chorus. The Evangelist describes the burial. The Jews ask Pilate to make the grave sure.

77. Soli with Chorus. A soloist begins, 'And now the Lord to rest is laid,' and the choir answers, 'Lord Jesu, fare Thee well.'

78. CHORUS. Bach sums up :

In tears of grief, dear Lord, we leave Thee,
Hearts cry to Thee, O Saviour dear.
Lie Thou softly, softly here.
Rest Thy worn and bruised Body.
At Thy grave, O Jesu blest,
May the sinner, worn with weeping,
Comfort find in Thy dear keeping,
And the weary soul find rest.
  Sleep in peace,
Sleep Thou in the Father's breast.

APPENDIX I

THE CHORUS *He guilty is of death* (no. 42), with the 1911 translation, is given overleaf. See p. 43.

CORO I
Soprano
He guil - ty is of death,
Alto
He guil - ty
Tenor
He guil - ty is
Bass
He
CORO II
Soprano
Alto
Tenor
Bass

is of death,
of death,
guil - ty is of death,
f
He guil - ty is of death,
f
He guil - ty is
f
He guil - ty

He guil - ty is of
He guil - ty is of death,
He guil - ty
of death,
He guil - ty is of death,
is of death,

cresc.
ff
sf
death, He is guil - ty of death.
is guil - ty of death.
is of death, He is guil - ty of death.
of death, is guil - ty of death.
of death, is guil-ty, guil - ty of death.
He guil-ty is of death.
is guil-ty of death.
He is guil-ty, guil - ty of death.

APPENDIX II

NOTES FOR THE KEYBOARD PLAYERS

CONDUCTORS will find that they can save time by drawing up lists of instructions in advance, and handing them to the keyboard players at rehearsal. The following specimen lists are given in a condensed form ; for actual use, they should be so laid out that each movement has a line to itself. They incorporate the main recommendations made on pp. 31–53.

It must again be emphasized that these are recommendations and nothing more ; Bach's intentions are not known for certain.

Notes for the Harpsichordist

Play for the Evangelist (except, as instructed below, in nos 71 and 73) : the minor characters (except, as instructed below, the False Witnesses in no. 39 and the Two Priests in no. 50) : and the other movements listed below :

PART I

10, Da Capo from C : 12, 19 : 26, with Tenor Solo and Oboe (Orchestra I).

PART II

36, with Contralto (Orchestra I) : 39, not with the False Witnesses : 40 : 41, plain full chords according to the figuring : 50, not with the Two Priests : 51 : 61, Da Capo from one bar after C : 66, plain full chords :

70, with Contralto (Orchestra I) : 71, not in bars 10–12 : 73, bars 11–18 and 21–end : 75, Da Capo from fourth (or fifth) bar after C.

Notes for the Organist

Play for the part of Jesus and as follows :

PART I

1, support the chorale. Diminuendo four bars from end ; finish *ppp* : 3, 5, 7 : 9, manuals only : 14 : 15, with Jesus and choir : 16, 18, 21, 23 : 24, with Jesus. 32-foot in last five bars : 25, with Tenor Solo, manuals only, *pp*. Fill in essential harmony notes in bars 18, 21, and 22, as unobtrusively as possible : 26, with choir : 28 : 29, Da Capo from C : 31 : 33, begin with the fugue, letter C ; play in bars 2–5 after C ; reserve reeds for *ff* entry at F : 35, support the chorale.

PART II

36, with choir : 38 : 39, with False Witnesses : 42, with Jesus and choir : 43, with choir : 44 : 45, with choir : 47, 48 : 49, with choir : 50, with Two Priests : 53 : 54, with choir ; *fff* for 'Barabbas' : 55, 57 : 59, with choir : 60 : 62, with choir : 63, for verse 1 only : 65 : 67, with choir : 69 : 70, with choir : 71, with Jesus (bars 7–9), Evangelist (bars 10–12), and choirs : 72, tacet : 73, bars 1–10, 18–21 : 74, pedals only, *ppp* : 76, with choir : 77, 78.

APPENDIX III

An Authentic Continuo Realization

THE FRAGMENT of MS. reproduced overleaf is a continuo realization by Bach for the bass aria *Empfind' ich Höllenangst und Pein* in Cantata no. 3, *Ach Gott, wie manches Herzeleid*. There is no figured continuo part for this cantata.

The reproduction has been made by kind permission of Otto Haas Esq., not from the MS. itself, but from a plate in the auction catalogue of 21–2 Nov. 1930 issued by Messrs Liepmannsohn of Berlin.

The realization was evidently intended not for the harpsichord, but for the high-pitched organ of those times, since it is in E minor, whereas the aria is in F sharp minor.

In the transcription that follows on p. 73 the treble clef has been used instead of Bach's soprano clef, and the vocal part (transposed into E minor) has been added. The asterisks mark passages where there is some doubt about Bach's intentions.

Our thanks are due to Dr. Aber for translating the inscription by Professor Fischhof.

A genuine autograph of Joh. Seb. Bach given to me by Hauser and remarkable for the fact that Bach wanted to set an example for the organist of how he would have to accompany arias and realize the figured basses. The aria is from the motet *Ach Gott, wie manches Herzeleid* and is Part 4 (Bass Aria).

Prof. Fischhof

23.4.850

APPENDIX IV

Books for Further Reading

C. H. H. PARRY *Johann Sebastian Bach.* Putnam, 1909.

ALBERT SCHWEITZER *J. S. Bach.* English translation, Breitkopf, 1911 ; Black, 1923.

PHILIPP SPITTA *Johann Sebastian Bach.* English translation, Novello, 1884.

C. S. TERRY *Bach : The Passions, II.* Oxford University Press, *Musical Pilgrim* Series.

W. G. WHITTAKER *Fugitive Notes on Certain Cantatas and the Motets of J. S. Bach.* Oxford University Press, 1924. This book does not deal with the Passion itself, but discusses principles, and gives practical hints, that apply just as much to the Passion as to the Cantatas.

E. DANNREUTHER *Musical Ornamentation.* Novello.

ARNOLD DOLMETSCH *The Interpretation of the Music of the XVIIth and XVIIIth Centuries.* Novello and Oxford University Press.

R. DONINGTON *On Interpreting Early Music. Music and Letters,* July 1947.

C. S. TERRY *Bach's Orchestra.* Oxford University Press, 1932.

D. F. TOVEY *Essays in Musical Analysis : Chamber Music.* Oxford University Press, 1944. The main principles of continuo realization have probably never been stated as clearly and in as few words as on pp. 4–8 of this book. But for serious work of this kind it is essential to consult

F. T. ARNOLD *The Art of Accompaniment from a Thorough-Bass*. Oxford University Press, 1931.